A PIECE OF THE
PUZ LE

Z

Best Wishes
Coach [illegible]

Also from the Boys Town Press

Competing with Character®

The 100-Yard Classroom

Teaching Social Skills to Youth, 2nd Edition

Basic Social Skills for Youth

Common Sense Parenting®

Common Sense Parenting® DVD Series
- Building Relationships
- Teaching Children Self-Control
- Preventing Problem Behavior
- Correcting Misbehavior
- Teaching Kids to Make Good Decisions
- Helping Kids Succeed in School

Adolescence and Other Temporary Mental Disorders DVD

Changing Children's Behavior by Changing the People, Places, and Activities in Their Lives

A PIECE OF THE PUZ LE

Eight Traits of a Quality Teammate

KEVIN KUSH, M.A.

A Piece of the Puzzle

Published by the Boys Town Press
14100 Crawford St.
Boys Town, NE 68010

ISBN 978-1-934490-46-4

Boys Town Press is the publishing division of Boys Town, a national organization serving children and families.

Publisher's Cataloging-in-Publication Data

Kush, Kevin

A piece of the puzzle : eight traits of a quality teammate / written by Kevin Kush. -- Boys Town, NE : Boys Town Press, c2013.

1p. ; cm.

ISBN: 978-1-934490-46-4

Summary: Author and coach Kevin Kush outlines eight traits that can turn any group or organization into a cohesive, high performing team. Learn how selfless behavior, respect, resiliency, adaptability, feedback, energy, accountability, and a "we before me" attitude can lead to greater productivity and success. -- Publisher.

1. Organizational effectiveness. 2. Teams in the workplace. 3. Organizational behavior. 4. Labor productivity. 5. Success in business. 6. Self-help techniques. I. Title.

HD66 .K87 2013

658.4/022--dc23 1302

10 9 8 7 6 5 4 3 2 1

THIS BOOK IS DEDICATED TO...

To Dr. Dan Daly, Boys Town executive vice president director of youth care, your continued support of our Boys Town athletic programs does not go unnoticed. Your efforts made this book idea a reality. Thank you for being a piece of the puzzle!

ACKNOWLEDGMENTS

I would like to thank Mike Sterba for giving me the confidence to be a writer.

To my wife, Lynne, and sons, Keegan and Christian, everyday I thank God for the gift of our incredible family. We are an unbeatable team!

To my mother, Viola, the toughest person I know. Your unconditional love has made me the man I am today.

To my sister, Joanie, thank you for being a second mother to my boys!

Finally, to my Savior and Lord Jesus Christ, Thank you for today!

TABLE OF CONTENTS

INTRODUCTION

Excellence in any group can only be achieved when all the pieces fit together.

Introduction

When I was a child, my family spent a portion of each summer at a lakeside cabin in Minnesota. As if fishing, swimming, and boating weren't enough, my mother believed it was essential for us to spend any downtime putting together a jigsaw puzzle. Yes, that's right, a jigsaw puzzle! A three-, four-, or five-hundred piece puzzle that when fully assembled reflected a beautiful mountain scene or the inside gears of a clock. As a young boy, the puzzle represented monotony in a box, and suffice to say I wasn't exactly thrilled about it.

Within the first couple of days after arriving at the cabin, I would hear the sound of card table legs being unfolded and I immediately knew the puzzle process was about to begin. My mom would toss all of the puzzle pieces out on the table and enthusiastically proclaim, "It's time to get started!"

For the remainder of the week, my mom and I would periodically work on trying to get all of the cardboard pieces to look like whatever was on the outside of the puzzle box. If it happened to be raining, I was stuck inside toiling away on the project for much longer than I wanted. (When I told this story to my teenage sons, they immediately asked, "Why would you want to do that?" I must admit I didn't have a good answer for them!)

Toward the end of the week, I always found myself more energized to work on the puzzle and I would put in more time and effort to get it finished. After all, the pile of individual pieces was almost gone and the ones we put together were actually resembling something pretty cool.

On more than one occasion, as the puzzle quest was drawing to an end, the unthinkable occurred: One piece was missing! (I would always blame my father for hiding the all-important hunk of cardboard. He was a notorious practical joker who wasn't beyond this kind of trick.) When we couldn't locate the missing piece, I found myself bothered the puzzle would remain incomplete. There was a fascinating or beautiful creation sitting on the table, but that one missing piece marred the image and the time and effort we put into the puzzle. It just didn't feel as satisfying and fulfilling to have an incomplete puzzle, even it was only one missing piece.

The football team I coach and the group or organization you are part of are much like that jigsaw puzzle. We also need all the pieces to be complete in order to excel and be successful. On my team, the puzzle pieces are my players. In your organization, the puzzle pieces are the employees. If you are part of a civic group, the puzzle pieces are your members.

When a group is struggling and performing poorly, the problem usually results from pieces that are not fitting together correctly. Excellence in any group can only be achieved when all the pieces fit together. That's why each person must assume the responsibility of being the best "teammate" or puzzle piece he or she can be.

Coaching Pieces of the Puzzle

Over the last two and a half decades, I've been a high school football coach and teacher. I spent my first nine years as a football coach and business education teacher at a large public high school in

Omaha, Nebraska. During my time there, we won many games, including a state championship, and we were a perennial powerhouse.

In 1996, I became the head football coach at Boys Town High School. The centerpiece of Boys Town's work with kids is its residential care program located on its Home Campus in the Village of Boys Town, Nebraska. Kids who come here are often unmotivated and usually academically, behaviorally, and/or emotionally challenged. At Boys Town, boys and girls live separately in homes in a family-style environment where married couples provide the warmth, structure, and teaching necessary to allow healing to take place. The campus includes a high school and middle school, both with full athletic as well as academic programs. While some youth live at Boys Town for many years and graduate from high school here, the average length of stay for a boy or girl is about eighteen months. This creates a unique challenge when trying to build a successful team year in and year out.

When I became Boys Town's football coach, my biggest challenge was not to teach my players the game of football; rather, it was getting them to work together as a team. I quickly realized that for our team to reach its potential and succeed, I had to teach each player how to be a great teammate.

In 2005, I had the honor of representing Boys Town on ABC's World News Tonight as the "Person of the Week." I remember talking with one of the ABC crewmembers who was on Boys Town's campus filming the news story. The interviewer asked me, "What do you hope these young men take away from their experience of playing football at Boys Town?" Without hesitation, I said, "I hope our kids have learned how to be a piece of the puzzle."

Over the past sixteen years, I have managed a football program at Boys Town that has enjoyed a great deal of success. We have won 129 games while losing only 40. The football team has consistently finished in the top 10 in the state of Nebraska and has done so with players who have little or no athletic background. In fact, many of our players have never been on an organized team of any type! I attribute a big part of our good fortune and accomplishments to the fact that our coaching staff spends a great deal of time teaching our players how to be good teammates.

Some of you reading this might be thinking, "But, Coach, you're talking about dealing with kids." That's true. But do you know what adults are? That's right — big kids! As adults, we bring some of the same problems and issues to the table as kids do. Think about all the "teams" (family, work, community, etc.) that you are currently a member or part of. I bet you can come up with people who are never willing to pitch in and help because, according to them, "It's not my job." I bet you know people who do not get along well with others like fellow coworkers or group members. I bet you can recall situations where a person pouted or argued when given feedback from an authority figure. And I bet you can picture individuals who are consistently pessimistic and negative. You get the idea here. Adults often struggle just like kids do in being a good teammate.

Become a Piece of the Puzzle!

Becoming an effective piece of the puzzle is what this book is all about. In the following chapters, I will discuss the eight traits I have found essential for individuals to learn and exhibit in order for their "team" to consistently be productive and successful.

As you read through the eight traits, think about where you are at with each one and give yourself a grade. Do a personal evaluation by asking yourself the following: "In which areas am I strong? Which areas need attention and improvement?" This will give you a baseline to work from and help you better understand your strengths and areas for development.

The eight traits are universal and apply to any group setting, whether you are an employee of a Fortune 500 company or a member of the local Optimist Club. What's important is that you learn what it takes to be a great teammate. So let's get busy working on making your puzzle complete!

1

BELIEVE IN THE TEAM CONCEPT

Change 'me thinking' into 'we thinking!'

CHAPTER 1

Believe in the Team Concept

Football is the ultimate team sport; eleven players must work in unison like a well-oiled machine. On offense, for example, the center must snap the ball correctly to the quarterback or the play fails. And the guard must make his block or the running back will be tackled in the backfield before he can get to the line of scrimmage. Each player has a specific job to do in order to maximize the team's chances of succeeding.

I regularly stress to my players that our team is made up of a bunch of individuals but that no one person is more important than all of us collectively. It is the team that achieves great things, not the individual.

And it's imperative that my players believe that. One of my main goals as a coach is to get individual players to change "me thinking" into "we thinking."

Your team is no different from mine. You, too, are a part of something bigger than yourself. When you believe in and are willing to buy into the team concept, you have taken the first step toward helping yourself and your team excel. The next step is to put that belief and willingness into action. The rest of the chapter discusses how you can go about doing that.

Nothing was Ever Accomplished Alone

Can you think of something significant in your life that you accomplished all by yourself, without any assistance from others? Let me speed things up for you: You can't! When my fifth-grade project won the science fair, my mom helped me paint the poster board for the display. If it wasn't for the help and encouragement of my teachers in high school, I'm not sure I would have graduated. In college, I was recognized as the outstanding business education student in the state of Nebraska, but it was my sister who helped me get to that point by teaching me organization skills and study habits. And I landed the head-coaching job at Boys Town because the coach I had previously worked for taught me the ins and outs of how to run a successful football program. Author and leadership expert John Maxwell said it well: "Even the Lone Ranger had Tonto." This is true for all of us in any of our endeavors.

Most people know Alexander Graham Bell invented the telephone, but not many have heard of Benjamin Bredding. He was the bright electrician who helped Bell set up the world's first two-way long distance telephone apparatus. Bell's knowledge of electricity was very limited and he needed Bredding's help to succeed. Also, Charles Lindberg was the first aviator to fly nonstop from New York to Paris. He was a national and international hero, and he made air travel a viable source of transportation. However, had it not been for the nine St. Louis businessmen who financed the cost of his plane, this historic and transformational feat would never have taken place. Both Bell and Lindberg are credited with these remarkable accomplishments but they did not do them alone!

I'm sure your team has accomplished some great things — some big and some not so big. Over the course of these achievements, others were involved in some form or fashion to help make things work out well. Thinking you can go it alone is unwise and a surefire way to fail. I have yet to witness a person who has won some type of award approach the podium and say, "I have no one to thank. I did this all by myself."

There is Power in Numbers

When I speak to groups, I often like to illustrate the "power of we" by playing a game. I randomly select a person from the audience, place him or her in front of the group, and explain that we are going to have a contest involving the individual against the group. I then randomly select a card from a stack of "task cards," each of which describes a different activity. For example, a card might read "play the piano," "install a ceiling fan," or "clean a catfish." If anyone in the room is proficient at the specific task, he or she raises a hand and the group is awarded a point. If the individual knows how to perform a task, he or she is awarded a point. I keep a running tally for both the group and individual. As the game progresses, the inevitable occurs: The group scores more points than the individual by a wide margin. This helps to demonstrate there is tremendous power in numbers.

Only once has an individual won at the game. A few years ago, a young woman who was pitted against the group said she could do every task I read. She could "spin a clay pot," "skydive," and "train a hunting dog." It was amazing! This multitalented person completely destroyed my example. The entire time I could not help but think that she was going to make some young man very happy…or possibly quite miserable!

On your team, you are surrounded with different types of people, each possessing unique gifts, talents, and skills. Be smart and tap into them! The more people on your team, the larger your team's "portfolio of talents." As the English writer John Heywood wrote, "Many hands make work light." More does not always and automatically mean better, but it is important for you to understand that your team can greatly benefit from utilizing others' talents.

Firefighter Efficiency

My father was a member of a special team: He was a captain on the Fire Department for the city of Omaha. Dad would describe to me how the truck would roll up to a fire and each man would exit the rig with a purpose and sense of urgency. Every man had a responsibility and specific job to do. For example, one firefighter would open a fire hydrant, two others would lay down hose, and another group of three would set up ladders. Every task was specific and important, and every second was critical — there was no time for debate! Each firefighter on my dad's crew was dependent on the others. Every team should strive to operate with "firefighter efficiency."

For this to happen, each team member must swallow his or her pride and check his or her ego at the door. I'm sure you've heard the expression, "There is no 'I' in 'team.'" It is true! Team members should not get caught up in who does what, what is fair and equal, and who gets credit. What matters most is doing the task in front of you to the best of your ability so the team can successfully reach its goals.

I Need You!

My coaching staff is made up of myself and five other assistant coaches. I need and depend on each and every one of them. Each coach is responsible for a crucial part of our program and team. They have specific duties involving offense, defense, special teams, strength and conditioning, video coordination, and others. I oversee all of this but aspire not to micromanage (which I believe could really be called "psycho-managing").

It is important for you to find and hire good team members and then let them do their jobs. Also, take time to tell them they are important and crucial to the team's success. There are always opportunities and many different ways to let people know they are important. One of the best ways to do this is by writing personal notes. The power of a handwritten, personal note is incredible and much more powerful than a text or email.

Each year at the end of our football season, I buy a box of thank-you cards and write and send a personal note to each coach and to other individuals who helped contribute to our success. I've found that these notes have a profound, positive effect on people. They appreciate being acknowledged in such a personal way. Give it a try! Take out a pen and put your thoughts about your teammates on paper. Let them know how important they are to you and the team!

2

EXHIBIT SELFLESS BEHAVIOR

A good teammate will sacrifice personal gain for the benefit of the group.

CHAPTER 2

Exhibit Selfless Behavior

The ability to put the team's benefit ahead of personal gain is something I want all of my players to learn and display. Unfortunately, it seems to be getting harder and harder to get individuals to buy into this quality. Mainstream society conveys a very clear message to kids and adults: "Get yours!" That's why many group leaders feel like they are fighting an uphill battle. Getting people to exhibit selfless behavior isn't an easy proposition in today's world.

I believe a good deal of this selfish way of thinking and behaving came out of the 1980's, which is commonly referred to as the "me" decade. At that time, many self-help books and experts encouraged people to exult the self, climb the corporate ladder to success, and not worry about who you stepped on along the way. Two highly popular television shows during this time were *Dynasty* and *Dallas*. Both were centered on greed and the accumulation of wealth at any cost. And the term "yuppie," which was used to describe young urban professionals who were upwardly mobile, was born at that time. The message was loud and clear: Getting what you wanted was the ultimate goal.

This message continues to influence people and impact how they interact within groups and teams. It takes a lot of effort from leaders to combat this self-centered way of thinking. Getting teammates to sacrifice personal achievement for the group's benefit is a vital objective if you want your team to be successful. The rest of this chapter discusses how to go about cultivating a selfless mindset on your team.

Do the Grunt Work

The term "grunt work" refers to tasks on a team that are difficult, not much fun, and definitely not glamorous. Every group needs individuals who are willing to jump in, get their hands dirty, and do whatever it takes to get the job done. The more people are willing to pitch in and do grunt work, the easier it is to achieve success.

An example of this is the story of Dan Ruddiger, a Notre Dame football walk-on who inspired the movie *Rudy*. Ruddiger was willing to do the grunt work as a scout team player. This meant each week during the season he helped to simulate the opponent's offense and defense against the top units. It also meant he came to practice every day and got the snot beat out of him! But Ruddiger's contributions were critical to getting the team prepared for success on game day. And he did this thankless task with gusto and effort. He put the team ahead of himself.

On my Boys Town football team, we give an award each week to the top scout team player. It's become the most prestigious award a player can win on our team. The person who earns the award has the honor of leading our team onto the field before a game while carrying a giant flag emblazoned with the Boys Town Cowboy star — our team logo. Scout team players work their tails off throughout the week in practice to earn this honor. It's a way we teach our kids the importance of being a selfless teammate.

You and your team members can focus on doing the grunt work just like Rudy and my scout team players by being willing to...

- **Arrive early**
- **Stay late**
- **Make a pot of coffee in the morning for the group**
- **Clean up a mess someone left**
- **Set up tables and chairs for a meeting and then put them away afterwards**
- **Help a coworker finish a project**

Any team or group always has plenty of grunt work that needs to be done. All you have to do is keep your eyes open and contribute when you see the opportunity. You'll find that when you do, others will follow your lead.

It's Not About You

You won't drive by a Macy's® or Walmart® retail store and see the name of an employee on the outside of the building. And when the Indianapolis Colts won the Super Bowl in 2007, the score broadcasted to the world was not Peyton Manning (the Colts' superstar quarterback at the time) 29 and the Chicago Bears 17.

Successful teams are made up of individual members who allow the team to take center stage. They understand it's not about them; it's about the group.

Many of my players lack this trait when they first try out for the team. They think it's all about individual glory, and getting their name in the newspaper is their major priority. Playing on the offensive line or kickoff squad doesn't appeal to them. Instead, they want to be a quarterback, running back, or receiver who scores touchdowns.

A few years ago, a young man told me he had to play a position where he could score touchdowns because he had a great end zone dance. That's the exact kind of mentality we have to work hard to change with many of our players. One of the first things we tell players is, "It's not about you." These four simple words teach players to begin thinking in terms of the team concept.

We also teach them it's about "we" and not "me." We stress they are representing the team and the Boys Town community as a whole. The goal is to get them to think about the bigger picture — team, family, and community. It takes dedication and persistence to get players to do this but it's vital to our success.

Not everyone on a team can be a leader or superstar, whether that's on my team or your team. The vast majority of responsibilities and tasks on any team are not flashy and don't result in a bunch of attention or adulation. They mostly involve ordinary, behind-the-scenes work. However, this is just as critical to a team's success as the efforts of those who get more of the limelight. Leaders should strive to convey the team concept to their members and let them know that all work done on a team is equally important.

One way you can do this is to have the phrase "It's not about you!" printed on cards or hung on the wall in a common area. It can help remind people about the team-first mentality. This can help individuals to think before they complain about their role or task, or act in ways that might be detrimental to the group.

I am not suggesting that individual concerns aren't relevant. Of course they are. The point here is there are many times when decisions are made that are in the best interest of the group and not the individual. This isn't always easy for members to deal with but it's necessary for team unity and success.

Don't Worry Who Gets Credit

Legendary UCLA basketball coach John Wooden said, "It is amazing how much can be accomplished if no one cares who gets the credit." He coached UCLA to ten NCAA national championships in a twelve-year span so he knows something about how to help a team achieve. Coach Wooden knew that for his team to reach its full potential, he had to have players who were not concerned about always being honored and praised for individual success.

It continually amazes me to hear about teams that are enjoying a ton of success, yet have individuals who are unhappy. Often, these people say things like:

- **"We won the game but coach didn't mention me in the newspaper."**
- **"The presentation went great but my boss told Jane she did a great job and not me."**
- **"We got the problem resolved and the customer was happy but it was my idea and nobody knows it."**

People who need to be recognized for everything they do make poor team members. The people you want on your team are ones who show maturity, are concerned only about moving the team forward, and are enthusiastic about doing what it takes to make the team better.

In 1996, I took over the Boys Town football program. The year prior to my arrival, the team hadn't won a game. I was able to help turn things around in a hurry — we won one game my first year! All joking aside, we were awful. The second year, things started to improve and we had an opportunity to make the state playoffs. During that season, one of my starting receivers asked if he could visit with me after practice. He was upset that our running back and quarterback were getting most of the attention and credit for our team's good fortune. My first thought, which I thankfully kept to myself, was, "You have got to be kidding me!" Instead, I calmly told the young man we could easily solve his dilemma: All he had to do was turn in his football equipment and the second-string receiver would become the starter. The young man knew I meant what I said and he left my office without saying another word. The message was loud and clear: Individual acclaim doesn't matter, team success does. To the young man's credit, he took this to heart and did a heck of a job for us the rest of the year without any more complaints.

All of us enjoy being acknowledged when we do something well. Good coaches, managers, and leaders know this and do give recognition for jobs well done. It's important to understand, however, that when you are part of a team, there will be many times when your work will go unrecognized. When this happens, deal with it in a positive and mature way by asking yourself, "Is the team having success?" If that is the case, then pat yourself on the back because that's what really counts!

Would you rather be a member who receives a bunch of accolades on a losing, underachieving team or an unsung member of a successful, overachieving team? If the answer is the latter, then you are one of those selfless people who would be an asset to any team, group, or organization. And you are the type of person I'd like on my team any day!

3

RESPECT EVERYONE

In the absence of respect, teammates are more likely to create a "tug-of-war" climate where individuals work against each other instead of with each other.

CHAPTER 3

Respect Everyone

It was the night before the start of fall football practice a few years ago and I was having trouble falling asleep because I was excited about the upcoming season. My returning Boys Town team was loaded with talent. We had a very real chance of winning a state championship, which hasn't happened at Boys Town in the decades since the start of the modern state playoff era. At the start of the season, expectations and spirits were high.

During the following ten weeks of the season, everything unraveled and came crashing down. We never came close to reaching our potential and goals.

The biggest factor behind our demise was the lack of respect players showed one another. At seemingly every turn, players tore each other down instead of supporting, building up, and encouraging each other. There was conflict in the locker room, tension and finger pointing at practice, and even fights on the field. As coaches, we addressed and taught alternative, positive ways to interact; but the players were stuck in a cycle of disrespect. In the end, this destroyed a promising team and chance for a historic season.

It is very difficult, if not impossible, for every person on a team to like all of his or her teammates. That's just human nature. And it doesn't automatically lead to a team's downfall. What can cause that to happen is when team members, like my football players that year, don't put effort into valuing each other and their common goals. When respect is absent, teammates are more likely to create a "tug-of-war" climate where individuals work against each other instead of with each other.

All teams, groups, and organizations have common goals that are shared by their members. To reach these goals, it's imperative for everyone to put away personal differences and strive to create an atmosphere rich in respect and mutual cooperation. In this chapter, we will explore ways to cultivate this type of environment.

Everyone Affects Team Morale

This chapter is titled "respect everyone" for a reason. It is not titled "show respect only to those who are on the same level on the organizational chart or to those who make the same amount of money." The emphasis here is on everyone. Why? Because each person has a direct impact on what kind of culture and atmosphere you have on your team.

Early in my career, I was an assistant football coach at a large suburban high school. The head coach there would have a "seniors only" cookout before each season. The objective of the gathering was to build team unity, set some goals for the upcoming season, and of course eat a meal together (which teenage males love to do!). After eating, each senior was required to speak in front of the group about what he planned to contribute to the team. Most players rambled on about how many yards they were going to gain, what post-season honors they would earn, what scholarships they would be awarded, and other individual accomplishments. Very few talked about the team.

At one of these get-togethers, as things were about to wrap up, one young man I didn't recognize slowly stood up and walked to the front to address the group. Have you ever had that uneasy feeling before someone speaks to a group that it's not going to go well? Well, I had that feeling that night with this young man. I looked down at my shoes, trying not to look at anyone. I did make eye contact with the head coach and silently mouthed, "Who is that?" My boss shrugged his shoulders as if to say, "I have no clue." You see, not one of the coaches knew who this kid was. He had not been with the team all summer, lifting weights, running, or participating in our off-season activities. Yet here he was, getting ready to take his turn addressing the team.

He introduced himself as Adam, then said, "I spent the last three years in the stands watching you guys play because I was scared. Not anymore! I am getting out of my comfort zone and am coming out for football. I want to know what it feels like to run out on the field in a uniform. I know I am not one of the best players but I can guarantee you this: I will show up on time for every practice, do everything the coaches ask of me, and cheer for you guys as loud as I can." Then he quietly sat back down. I could barely keep from giving Adam a standing ovation.

As the season progressed, Adam did all the things he said he would do. He made the best use of his talents to help the team succeed. He was dead on about one thing: He certainly wasn't one of the best players. But that didn't matter because Adam had a very positive and profound effect on team morale and chemistry, which is every bit as important as throwing, running, catching, and tackling.

At one particularly tough practice when many players were on the verge of quitting, Adam was the one encouraging everyone to "just keep going." He brought this same upbeat attitude to every practice, workout, and game. Whatever he was asked to do, Adam did it with energy and without complaint. His attitude was infectious to others on the team even though he was far from one of our best players and rarely played in games. But, he had the same kind of impact on the team that any starter had.

That season we won the state championship. In my basement, I have a large framed picture of that team. Many of the players went on to play at the collegiate level and one even played in the National Football League. Every time I see the picture, my eyes are drawn not to the superstars but to a young man in the front row — Adam. He's a great example of how every team or group member can have an impact on building the morale and chemistry needed for a team to succeed.

You Fight Harder for a Friend

What would you do if a good friend called in the middle of the night and said, "My car broke down on the highway. I need your help." Most likely you would be out the door and in your vehicle so quickly you might forget to put on your shoes or grab your keys. Why so frantic? Because your friend is in need and you care.

What if you brought just a fraction of this kind of caring approach to your team, group, or organization? Do you think things would be different? Absolutely they would! Because you work and fight harder for a friend. When team members enjoy being around each other, communication improves, blaming and finger pointing decreases, and productivity soars.

The million-dollar question is how to foster this type of unity on your team. Presidents, CEOs, coaches, and other leaders have been seeking the answer to this forever. The complete answer is complex and unique for each group, but I believe it all starts with respect. When teammates show respect to each other, it generally results in them caring about one another. Nowhere is this more evident than with the men and women in our armed forces.

In his book, *We Were One*, historian Patrick O'Donnell followed the 1st Marine Regiment as the soldiers fought their way into and through the city of Fallujah in Iraq. O'Donnell describes the respect soldiers had for each other and the unifying bond that created as a team. This respect and unity was developed from the grueling and abundant training they did together before their deployment. During that time, soldiers got to know one another on deeper levels, strengthening relationships. Then when they were in combat together in Fallujah and their lives depended on each other, the soldiers admitted to O'Donnell that their main motivation for operating at a high level was for their fellow soldier. Numerous soldiers said it was all about "the man on my right and the man on my left." This is proof positive that you do indeed fight harder for a friend!

The closer teammates are, the more likely they are to take the team to the next level — where everyone is fully invested physically, mentally, and emotionally.

Develop Unity

If you are a leader of a team, group, or organization, it's your responsibility to work on developing unity. Start by establishing performance levels and standards that people know and clearly understand. And when you see behaviors that are harmful to unity building (bullying, gossiping, etc.), address them right away. Developing unity starts at the top so make it a priority to model it every day. When you treat people with respect, it has a trickle down effect on others.

Developing unity on my Boys Town football teams is always a daunting task. My players come from different parts of the country and didn't grow up together like many of the young men we compete against. That's why I like to do many team-building activities. Going to a movie, playing kickball, or just having a meal together is an opportunity for teammates to learn more about each other, develop friendships, and begin to really know and care for each other.

These same kinds of activities can work on any team. The list of things to do to build unity is endless, so be creative. For example, one company I worked with developed a "bragging board." It was a publicly placed bulletin board where employees could post pictures and stories they were proud of. One man posted a picture from his daughter's dance recital. A mother pinned up an announcement that her son was returning home from a tour of duty in Iraq. As time went on, team members learned new things about each other that they would have never known. When team members have the opportunity to learn a bit more about each other on a personal level, the results are stronger bonds and a more cohesive unit.

4

HANDLE ADVERSITY

When adversity hits, you can feel sorry for yourself and do nothing or you can choose to make the situation better.

CHAPTER 4

Handle Adversity

In your personal and professional life, it is not a question of if adversity will happen but when. This is one of life's guarantees and an inevitable part of being human. Many of my football players have experienced a great deal of adversity in their lives before coming to Boys Town and don't realize it. I like to "sell" them on the fact that they are experts at getting up when knocked down.

If you think about it, you really only have two choices when adversity strikes. You can do nothing and feel sorry for yourself; or you can choose to take actions to make the situation better. The choice is yours. However, if you desire to help move yourself and your team forward, it's imperative you take action and "get back on that bronco" when bucked off. As they say in rodeo circles, and as we use as a rallying cry with our Boys Town Cowboy football players, "Cowboy up!" It's easy to be energetic and upbeat when your team is on top. The true test of a person's character is how he or she reacts when times are tough. In this chapter, we'll discuss a few ways to do that.

"What an Opportunity!"

My son, Keegan, made the phrase "what an opportunity" come to life during his first year of high school. Keegan is a very quiet, reserved kid, and his social outlet is sports. During freshman football season, Keegan complained that his back was bothering him. My wife, Lynne, wanted him to see a sports doctor. I told Keegan to stretch his hamstrings and take a couple of Ibuprofen and that he would be fine. I honestly believed the pain was due to muscle soreness and was nothing serious.

When the season ended, Keegan continued to complain of back pain and it seemed to be getting worse. We took him to a doctor. After reviewing the results of a CAT scan, the doctor said, "Coach, your son has been playing football with a broken back. He has two fractured vertebrae." I sheepishly looked at my wife and said, "Oops." There were some remarks Lynne made to me that I would rather not disclose; let's just say she was upset with me for not taking Keegan to the doctor sooner.

After the diagnosis, Keegan asked the doctor, "What do I have to do? Wrestling season is coming up." The doctor looked at Keegan with a serious look and said, "Son, you can't wrestle. The fact of the matter is that you will be wearing a back brace twenty-three hours a day for a while, and you are also going to wear an electronic bone growth stimulator to aid in the healing." The room went quiet. Then Keegan said, "What about running track in the spring?" The doctor said to come back in four months and he would take another CAT scan. After that, he would let Keegan know if he was cleared to participate in track.

At the follow-up appointment, the doctor informed Keegan that his back was not healed yet and track was not an option. For the first time in his teenage life, I witnessed Keegan break down and cry. I gave him some time to grieve. Later, I grabbed Keegan by the shoulders, looked him straight in the eye, and enthusiastically exclaimed, "What an opportunity!"

Living with a football coach, my wife and kids get to hear all kinds of catchy motivational phrases and quotes — whether they want to hear them or not. "What an opportunity" was not a foreign phrase to Keegan's ears. After I said it, he replied, "You always say that when things go bad. How is this an opportunity?" I told him, "You've always been a good student and this is your opportunity to be a great student. When the rest of the track team is going to practice, you can go to the library and study. Instead of putting in time on the track, you can put in time hitting the books. What better way to turn something negative into a positive?" After a few seconds of thought, Keegan said, "I can do that!" He was hooked on the idea.

Keegan enthusiastically set forth on his quest to be the best student he could be. Day after day, he would hustle to the library after school and stay until it closed. One day, he came home and appeared to be down in the dumps. I asked him what was wrong and he said, "Guys are making fun of me for going to the library every day and some are even making comments about my back brace being a turtle shell." I did my best to tell him to ignore those things and just stay the course. Keegan said he would but I could tell he was still bothered. I remember thinking to myself that turning a negative situation into a positive one is much harder than it sounds. And I truly hurt for my son.

Keegan continued to focus his efforts on academics through the end of the school year. A few days after school had ended, I was sitting in my favorite chair watching the evening news when Keegan came in from getting the mail. He calmly walked over to me and placed a sheet of paper in my lap. It was Keegan's grades. He had earned all A's and his class rank was number one out of 342 students! I looked up at him with a big smile. He looked me straight in the eye and said, "What an opportunity," and walked away.

As I sat holding the school transcript, I was overcome with emotion. Seven months earlier, Keegan was crying because of bad medical news and now it was his proud father shedding a few tears.

You, too, can tap into the power of this phrase. Make it into a big sign and hang it in an area of high traffic where people will see it often. Or write the words on an index card and tape it to the top of your computer. You could even put the letters "WAO!" on something you see everyday (a bathroom mirror at home, the banner on your cell phone, etc.) as a reminder to think of tough situations that arise during the day as opportunities. Simply thinking about or reciting a phrase like this can help give you the energy needed to keep plugging away until things get better — because they always do!

Control What You Can Control

In any adverse situation, there are things you can and can't control. I once worked with a coach who would worry like crazy whenever there was a forecast for bad weather on game day. He used up a lot of energy fretting about something he had no control over. When adversity rears its head, it is imperative you focus only on the variables you can have an impact on.

In the movie *Apollo 13*, shortly after the famous phrase, "Houston, we have a problem," is uttered, the scene moves to the control room where technicians and engineers are frantic. They are all talking and going off in different directions. The situation is brought back to order by the head of mission control when he says, "People, work the problem!"

Working the problem is exactly what needs to happen when you or your team experiences adversity. Don't waste time pointing the finger, laying blame, or worrying about factors outside of your control. Instead, channel your energy and efforts into taking actions that help to solve the situation that's in front you. Action is the key — and you certainly have control over that!

Get Back to Basics

When a team experiences hardship, team members look for answers to the same question: "What do we do now?" There is no exact blueprint to follow that answers this question for every adverse situation. I've found that a good rule of thumb to follow is to go back to the fundamentals — or the tried-and-true actions and activities that have helped your team have success. It's what I like to call "getting back to the basics."

In football, I know what basic areas my team must be proficient in to have success: blocking, tackling, and ball security. If we are losing games and facing adversity on the field, most times it can be traced back to the fact we are not performing well in these areas. I have found it best to focus my time and energy on these three areas instead of inventing new plays or moving players to different positions.

What are the basics that make your team successful? In business, it might be exceptional customer service or unmatched quality control. An athletic team might pride itself on tremendous conditioning. You can get to know your basics better by listing the fundamental principles your team adheres to and aspires to follow. Then when adversity hits, you know what basics your team needs to work on to right the ship.

5

ADAPT TO CHANGE

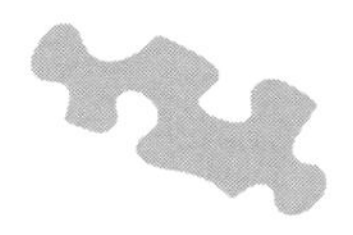

Your ability to adapt to both personal and professional change will impact the success or failure of your team.

CHAPTER 5

Adapt to Change

You have probably heard the expression "change is inevitable." When you are a member of a team, you can be certain that you will be confronted with change. If you are part of an organization, change might come in the form of new policies and procedures, the addition of new team members, or a shift in job responsibilities. Change is also an inevitable part of your personal life. You might start a new job or go back to school, have a change in your marital status, or move to a new city.

Your ability to adapt to changes like these will have a direct impact on whether you are successful navigating through them. Charles Darwin once said, "It is not the strongest of the species that survives, nor the most intelligent; it is the one that is most adaptable to change." In this chapter, we will address how to adapt to change, the role of the leader in managing change, and the importance of team members embracing change.

Leaders Must Manage Change

Not only is change inevitable but it's also scary. The older I get, the more frightening it is when I have to deal with change. Lets face it, most of us like things the way they are; it's comfortable and predictable. When change occurs, it disrupts our routine and throws our lives off balance. As a team leader, it's important to understand change causes anxiety to team members. Your job is to minimize that anxiety as much as possible by calmly navigating your team through the change process.

There has been a multitude of research conducted and literature written on the topic of change management. Opinions vary widely regarding the best way to manage change. Regardless of what school of thought you ascribe to and use, the important thing is to buy into something because change won't manage itself.

The worst thing a team leader can do is to toss change at team members without any warning or plan of action. That's like throwing a bucket of ice-cold water on them — it shocks the system and causes discomfort and pain. When change isn't managed at all or well, team members are less receptive and tend to reject it. When change is managed well, the jolt isn't as jarring and disruptive and team members are more open to it.

One way to approach your team about upcoming change is to keep them informed as much as possible about it and ask them, when appropriate, for their opinions. Many times, this is enough to lessen the impact and get them to buy into what's happening.

Once change is announced and implemented, it's important to keep your pulse on its effectiveness and answer any questions that might arise. Instituting change isn't a one-and-done proposition; rather, it is a long-term process. And it's up to team leaders to see the process through from start to finish.

When I became the head coach at Boys Town in 1996, I brought with me a ton of ideas I thought could improve the football program. In reality, it was a whole lot of change. All of my assistant coaches were holdovers from the previous head coach and used to doing things in specific ways. I knew that to get them on board with my system I would need to include them in the change process.

I met with all my assistants and listened to their input and opinions about the current state of the football program and how to best move forward. I asked them to discuss the program's strong points and areas where they thought things could be done differently and better. That fall, before implementing any change, I laid out on paper my ideas for the upcoming season and discussed them with my staff. Some of the changes came from their valuable input.

The coaches appreciated being involved in creating the new "blueprint" for our team's success. I told them if they had any problems with any aspect of the new procedures, they were welcome to come discuss them with me and that my door was always open. Throughout the year, I made a concerted effort to check on the effectiveness of the implemented changes. Looking back, I truly believe that my ability to manage that change effectively was a major factor contributing to our program's success.

Team Members Must Embrace Change

Noted sports psychologist Kevin Elko describes the place where people get together to complain and be negative as the "duck pond." We all know what goes on in the duck pond — a lot of quacking! This is generally what happens when change is announced and implemented on a team.

Initially, individuals are unhappy with change and look for others who feel the same way. The theme seems to be "let's be miserable together." While some people might consider this type of behavior a therapeutic form of venting, it does nothing to move the team forward.

There is an adage attributed to Henry Ford that states, "If you think you can or you think you can't, either way you are right." This is true of how you view change when it happens. The quicker you adopt a positive attitude and cast away negative ruminations, the sooner you will be able to see the intended benefits of change. One way to do that is to avoid (or quit) quacking and give change a chance.

Let's look at a couple of examples of what can happen when individuals and teams have the proper mindset about change.

From the Majors to the Minors and Back Again

In 2010, the Kansas City Royals professional baseball team decided that their number one draft pick from 2005, Alex Gordon, would help the organization more if he would change his position from third base to left field. Gordon had never played left field in the professional ranks. In order to learn all the intricacies of the outfield, Gordon was asked to take a demotion to their AAA farm club and reinvent himself.

Gordon embraced the change and saw it as a tremendous opportunity for himself and the team. After a stint in the minor league, Gordon returned to Kansas City in 2011 as their starting left fielder, won the American League Gold Glove award, and led major league baseball with twenty assists. By embracing change instead of resisting it, Gordon was able to make himself and the team better in new ways.

Domino's® Pizza

In 2008, Domino's Pizza underwent a complete facelift. Faced with low customer satisfaction and diminishing profits, the company reinvented its product and image. Domino's listened to its consumers' complaints and suggestions and went back in the kitchen to rebuild its pizza recipe from the crust up.

Company leaders implemented change on a number of different levels and employees embraced it. By 2010, Domino's showed an increase in sales of fourteen percent over the previous year. Customer loyalty improved tremendously and Domino's claimed a larger share of the always-competitive pizza market. Simply put, change saved the company from disaster.

As a member of a team, you will experience change so don't be surprised or caught off guard when it comes. Teams that successfully navigate change have leaders who are willing to implement and manage it and team members who embrace it. Initially, change is uncomfortable but it gets easier over time, and often it's the very thing individuals and teams need to move forward and succeed.

6

ACCEPT FEEDBACK

In order for you to improve at your job, whatever that job is, somebody has to give you feedback.

CHAPTER 6

Accept Feedback

As a football coach, my job requires me to communicate to players what they are doing wrong and how to make corrections. I also make a concerted effort to tell them what things they are doing properly and to keep doing them. Every season — and at times throughout the season — I tell my players their job is to accept feedback from coaches and implement it so they and the team can improve.

We have all gone through evaluations where our work or performance was judged or critiqued by someone else. This starts at a young age and continues into adulthood. It happens at home, in school, on teams, and in the workplace. In each of these settings, there are knowledgeable, experienced people skilled at examining performance and providing feedback. A key trait of a good team member is a willingness to put that feedback into action.

My teachers at St. Bridget's Grade School frequently gave me feedback on everything from good posture, how to properly stand in a line, and how to develop good penmanship. When I decided to play Little League baseball at the age of nine, my coach gave every team member feedback on hitting, base running, and fielding. At my first job working in a concession stand as a teenager, my supervisor evaluated everything from the taste of the lemonade I made to the cleanliness of the floor I swept.

Critique and criticism are still part of my life. Every year I am formally evaluated as a coach. And at home, my wife gives me feedback on a variety of issues! Feedback is an aspect of life one can't escape. Knowing how to accept and implement feedback is a vital part of being a successful team member and team. In this chapter, we'll talk about how to go about doing these things in ways that are productive for you and your team.

Feedback Is Your Friend

On Saturday mornings following Friday games, our football team and coaching staff meet to watch video of the previous night's contest. This is a tremendous opportunity for our team to get better through constructive feedback. During the meeting, we look at and critique every play numerous times. Coaches point out what players did correctly and where they need to improve. Our team gets an opportunity to see exactly how they performed. This critique session is as important to the players' and team's development and improvement as anything we do on the practice field — without it players would continue to make the same mistakes. That's why we teach players that feedback is their friend and not a foe.

The same can be true on your team. For you and your team to reach your potential and goals, feedback on performance is necessary. This might be done by a manger, supervisor, boss, team leader, coach, or other person in authority who is responsible for helping you improve your performance. This person may not have the luxury of watching you on video like I do with my football team, but he or she can observe you and provide you with what you need to succeed. Think of this person as someone who is concerned about you and cares about helping you improve. When you have that kind of attitude, feedback becomes an opportunity for learning and growth.

Say "Okay" and Implement the Feedback

It takes my high school players a bit of time to learn to listen when a coach is speaking and giving them feedback. We often have to remind them to do this, especially at the beginning of the season. Adults are no different. They, too, can struggle with listening to criticism. Legendary basketball coach Bobby Knight once said, "A lot of people hear, but not too many people listen."

Listening is a skill that requires concentration and effort. When someone is reviewing our work and providing constructive criticism, many of us have a tendency to tune out that person or try to explain our side of the story. When my players do this, we teach them to listen by remaining quiet and after given feedback, say, "Okay." We keep it very simple. If they want to explain or disagree, they can do so at a later time.

Listening and acknowledging feedback alone does not right the ship. You also must implement it and begin the process of change. Implementing feedback can be difficult. It usually requires you to change the way you have always done something. And it will likely take you out of your comfort zone, which means there will be discomfort and effort needed on your part. However, the long-term benefit you and your team will gain is worth a bit of short-term discomfort.

Have Rhino Skin!

I enjoy watching cable television networks like the "Discovery Channel" and "Animal Planet." My favorite episodes involve animals hunting and chasing down their prey. When one of these shows airs, I immediately call out to my two sons, "Get over here quick, one animal is eating another animal!" The next thing I usually hear is my wife sighing and saying something like, "There is way too much testosterone in this house." She is probably right.

You know what animal you never see being chased and taken down by another animal? The rhino. When harassed, the rhino just stands there and grunts at its attacker who then usually just backs down. Regardless of the surrounding mayhem, nothing seems to bother the rhino. You know why? Because the rhino has extremely thick skin that isn't easily penetrated or harmed.

When you receive feedback, do you have thick skin like the rhino or do you feel hurt and discouraged? Too many people allow feedback that is intended to help to penetrate their inner core. They internalize it and take it personally. This is not healthy or productive for anyone. When you're feeling sorry for yourself, it is difficult to focus on doing the things you need to do to help yourself and your team improve. Legendary football coach Lou Holtz said self-pity leads to self-destruction. I agree.

I have a small plastic rhino I keep on my desk to remind me to have thick skin, accept feedback, and not feel sorry for myself. One of the companies I spoke to informed me after my talk that they had purchased small plastic rhinos for their employees to remind them of the same thing. Try doing this for your team members, too! It's a great reminder that whenever feedback comes their way, the best way to handle it is to accept and implement it.

7

DEMONSTRATE HIGH ENERGY

No matter what talents God has given you, you control the level of energy and effort you demonstrate every day.

CHAPTER 7

Demonstrate High Energy

The following statement probably is no newsflash to you: People are not created equal. Even though it's not breaking news, it is a fact that some people are blessed with more natural ability than others in certain areas of life. For example, some people are faster, taller, and smarter than others. We all get dealt a hand of certain things we have little to no control over that we have to learn to accept and deal with. Regardless of the talents God has given you, one of the areas you do have control over is the level of energy and effort you demonstrate in your endeavors each day.

Ron Brown, an assistant football coach for the Nebraska Cornhuskers, tells his players that they are a "fraction." In order for a fraction to equal one-hundred percent, the numerator must equal the denominator. The denominator represents the skills people are born with — or the things they have no say in or control over (physical traits, the environment they were born into, etc.). The numerator represents the amount of energy and effort a person puts into the denominator every day. People are in complete control of the numerator. Brown says that for each player to maximize his abilities (or get the fraction to equal one-hundred percent), he has to "get his numerator up" every day. That is what this chapter is about — helping you learn how to get yourself and your team to demonstrate high energy on a daily basis.

Have Labrador Enthusiasm

I am an avid outdoorsman and share my love of the outdoors with my yellow Labrador retriever, Touchdown. (Yes, Touchdown is really my dog's name!) The thing I admire most about Touchdown and the entire Labrador breed is their enthusiastic demeanor. No matter the time of day or night, a Labrador is eagerly ready to take on the task at hand. It doesn't matter if it is four o'clock in the morning or afternoon. When I go to her kennel and open it up, Touchdown comes flying out ready and willing for whatever is next, whether that's a run with me, an outing to the hunting field, or a game of fetch in the yard.

People can get caught in a rut of crawling into and through their day with the energy of a slug, just waiting for the clock to strike quitting time. One of the keys to success is approaching your day with enthusiasm, ready to tackle whatever the day might bring. One way to do that is by trying to emulate the energy and excitement Touchdown brings to whatever is in front of her. She isn't concerned about what happened yesterday or what might happen tomorrow; instead, she is totally focused on the moment — and she's fired up about it!

A successful team member exhibits this same type of enthusiasm. Remember, enthusiasm is a choice — something you have total control over — so use it as much as possible. A team full of individuals with Labrador enthusiasm is tough to beat!

Avoid Moodiness

Generally speaking, when people ask you how you are doing, they really don't expect to hear the details of the current state of your life. Most of the time, people are simply being polite. They know you have problems just as they do but they don't expect you to discuss them. Instead, most of us courteously report that life is good and we avoid dumping on others, leaving that for another time with the appropriate people in our lives.

As a member of a team, it is important for you to bring your "A" game regarding your attitude and energy level. Nothing ruins team chemistry faster than team member's with poor moods and attitudes. That's why it is essential to leave personal problems out of the team environment.

Pat Summit, the long-time Tennessee Volunteers women's basketball coach, says this in her book, *Reach for the Summit*: "Moody people are rude people. They may even be a liability." I agree with this. I once worked for a manager who was extremely moody and he brought it into the workplace. If he was not happy, then no one could be happy. His erratic mood swings made everyone on the team uneasy and tense, and people were more concerned about what mood to expect each day than the tasks at hand. As a matter of fact, many of us would gather in the parking lot before work and "draw straws" to determine who would enter the office first to see if the boss was in a good or bad mood. On the occasions when I drew the short straw, I would reluctantly shuffle into work and make contact with our leader. A few minutes later, I'd return to the parking lot and flash my fellow employees a thumbs up or thumbs down sign to let them know what mood would permeate our work environment that day. As you can see, this is no way for a team to operate and it is no surprise that our team was not very productive.

How can you avoid bringing moodiness and a bad attitude to the team? One way that's worked well for me and my teams is discussed in the next section.

Fake It!

Some days it is not very exciting or much fun being part of a team. We all have days when physically and/ or mentally we don't feel our best. Perhaps we didn't get enough sleep or we're going through a stressful time in our personal lives. If we aren't careful, these issues can bleed over and have a negative impact on our team environments and teammates.

On my football team, I have a long-standing rule that helps to counter this. My coaches and players must adhere to the following rule at all times: When you really do not want to be here, just "fake it." It is that simple — and it works!

I tell players who are struggling to demonstrate high energy to pretend they are trying out for a part in a play. And the parts they are trying out for are enthusiastic football players. That means their task during practice is to fake it, ignore how they might really be feeling, and convince themselves and everyone around them that they are engaged and filled with energy. When practice is over, they can go out of character and back to feeling any way they want.

This can work for you and your team, too. On days you know it is going to be a struggle, give yourself a pep talk and reward yourself with something special if you can fake it throughout the day. Your pep talk might go like this: "I didn't get a good night's sleep but I am not going to let it affect my mood today. I am going to be full of energy for the duration of the day, and those who I come in contact with will not see my fatigue. After work, I am going to head home and reward myself with an afternoon nap."

When you are feeling one-hundred percent, exhibiting high energy is easy. The true test comes when you are dragging physically or emotionally. Recognizing you might have a difficult day is an important part of the solution. You may not have had a great deal of control over the circumstances that caused your funk but you do have control over how to get out of it. And it's your responsibility as a quality teammate to make the effort to do so. Teams that win have members committed to bringing their best everyday even when other parts of their lives aren't at their best.

8

BE ACCOUNTABLE

Take pride in your job and make sure you are in charge of what you are in charge of.

CHAPTER 8

Be Accountable

A few years ago, I had the opportunity to speak to the sales force of a large company at their annual convention. The theme of the conference was accountability. The message to team members was plain and simple: be accountable. I loved the theme and message. I really wasn't sure what it all meant to me but it sure sounded good. My whole life I had heard people use the word accountability and here it was again. On numerous occasions, I had even talked to my football teams about being accountable. But this conference made me put a lot more thought into what it really meant to be accountable.

On the plane flight home from the conference, I took out a legal pad to write down a description of what it meant to be an accountable team member. After filling three pages that really didn't say a whole lot, I ripped them up and started over. I knew an accountable teammate was someone who could be trusted and depended on. But I wanted it broken down into its simplest elements. The rest of this chapter discusses the elements I believe make up an accountable team member.

Do Your Job

Whether we are hired, appointed, or have volunteered, we all have a job to do on our teams. You might be a CEO, assistant coach, or committee chairperson. Every position — big and small — has certain responsibilities that go with it. To be an accountable team member means you carry out those responsibilities. It also means not wasting time and energy worrying about other people and how they do their job. Instead, your focus is squarely on doing your job as well as you can.

If your position has a job description available, I encourage you to review it. If you don't have one, pull out a sheet of paper and write one down on your own. Ask yourself these questions:

- **What purpose do I serve on the team?**
- **What tasks do I need to take care of on a daily, weekly, and/or monthly basis?**

Make a list and get organized. If you don't know the answers to any of these questions, ask your supervisor or co-workers. Knowing your job responsibilities makes it easier for you to do your job and to do it well.

Don't Make Excuses

Benjamin Franklin said, "He that is good for making excuses is seldom good for anything else." Those are pretty harsh words but they do ring true. The truth is few people want to hear why a job did not get done. Instead, they want people to follow through on their end. Excuse making is an attempt to justify poor performance and it can take down the whole team.

I once had a coach tell me that excuses are like armpits. Everybody has them and they all stink. That was a pretty graphic example but I got the message! As a high school football coach, I want my players to learn not to make excuses for their performance. It is a hard skill for kids (and adults) to master. Nobody likes to admit his or her performance was subpar — that he or she, in some fashion, dropped the ball. The remedy for this is to remember that everyone messes up. Mistakes are a part of life. The key is to admit when they happen and get on with looking for solutions.

Don't Blame Others

Another part of being accountable means taking responsibility for your actions and not blaming others. Excuses can sometimes come across as vague or fall into a gray area that can make it difficult to distinguish the reality of a situation. However, blaming someone makes it crystal clear that a person is deflecting accountability and responsibility by putting a face on poor performance. Many of us have blamed others at one time or another only to find out that it is the wrong way to go about handling a situation.

As a youth playing sports, I tried to blame others for my misfortune and mistakes on a number of occasions. In football, if I was tackled behind the line of scrimmage, it was because the offensive line did not block well enough. If I was pitching in Little League baseball and having trouble throwing strikes, it was because the umpire was making terrible calls. As soon as responsibility was shifted to another person, I could rest easy because it was not my fault. The problem with avoiding ownership was that my coaches and my father did not buy or accept it. They knew better and let me know in rather convincing ways that other people did not cause my problems or poor performance, and that blaming others was unacceptable.

When things do not go as planned on your team, blaming others creates tension and compounds frustration. It does nothing to solve the problem and negatively effects relationships with teammates. No one likes to be thrown under the bus. Shifting responsibility to another person sends a message that you are not responsible and don't hold other team members in high regard.

There is an old saying, "Anytime you point a finger at someone else, there are three fingers pointing back at you." I often tell my players to "point the thumb not the finger." By gesturing the thumb toward themselves and admitting they played a part in what went wrong, they are being accountable and doing their part in finding a solution. You, too, can make that part of your team.

PUTTING ALL THE PIECES TOGETHER

"The higher the ideal the more work is required to accomplish it. Do not expect to become a great success in life if you are not willing to work for it."

— Father Edward J. Flanagan, founder of Boys Town

CONCLUSION

PUTTING ALL THE PIECES TOGETHER

Never Underestimate the Impact You Have On Others

When you are a piece of the puzzle, you have an impact on everyone with whom you come in contact. From the time your feet hit the floor in the morning, you have a "thumbs up" or "thumbs down" effect on the people you interact with during the day. Your actions, words, gestures, and facial expressions convey either a positive or negative message. You can be a "sail" that helps your team move forward in a positive direction, or you can be an "anchor" that holds your team down. The choice is yours each and every day.

Let me share a good example of how to be a sail. When my youngest son, Christian, was in grade school, he had a teacher who did a great job of emphasizing the team concept with the class. Every class member was important and a piece of the puzzle. One of Christian's classmates was a boy named Austin who suffered from a profound intellectual and physical disability. Austin was confined to a wheelchair and could not speak, but he did try to communicate by making noises and sounds that were often disruptive to the class. The majority of the students did their best to not allow these disruptions to negatively impact the class or their day.

One day after school, Christian asked my wife, Lynne, and I if Austin could come over and play sometime. Lynne gave me a quizzical look and said, "Sure." Later when Lynne and I talked privately, I asked, "How are we going to make this happen?" My wife assured me it could be done and heaped praise on Christian for taking a step to make someone in his class feel wanted.

Lynne made contact with Austin's mother and a date was selected for Austin to come to our house. When the day arrived, Austin's mother was on time and told us she would need some help getting Austin inside. She first brought a large, soft blanket into our living room and laid it out on the floor. I then carried Austin's wheelchair into our house while his mother picked him up from his seat in the car and carried him inside. She laid Austin on the blanket along with some toys she had taken out of a backpack. Christian immediately joined Austin on the blanket and began showing him the toys. By the big smile on his face, it was obvious Austin was delighted to be playing with another kid.

What happened next I will not soon forget. I looked over and saw Austin's mother wiping away tears. We asked if she was okay and she proceeded to tell us that this was the first time her son had been invited to anything! She said that the phone call from my wife inquiring if Austin could be a guest in our home was one of the greatest surprises of her life. Christian's act of kindness had a very profound effect on a number of people that day.

When Christian and Austin returned to school the following day, Christian asked if he could permanently sit by Austin. Christian's presence next to Austin had a calming effect and other classmates began to stop by and say "hello" to Austin. Christian's actions showed me how one piece of the puzzle can help another piece of the puzzle fit in.

You, too, can make a difference on your team. During your day, there will be numerous opportunities for you to have a positive impact on others. The key is awareness. Have your radar up and be on the lookout for those moments. Then when they come, take action!

In football, the team that does the little things well generally comes out on top. It is no different on your team. A kind smile to a coworker, an offer to help with a project, a sympathetic ear to someone who is going through a difficult time, or just bringing someone a hot cup of coffee can have a huge, positive impact on your team.

The eight traits discussed in this book are meant to serve as a model for what a quality teammate looks like and sounds like. On my football team, we revisit these traits from time to time throughout the year. I have my players and coaches evaluate and grade themselves on each of the eight traits. They look at the ones they are strong in and also the ones that need attention. I encourage you and your team to do the same.

Achieving success on a team is never certain or easy. But having puzzle pieces that believe in the team concept, exhibit selfless behavior, have respect for others, handle adversity well, adapt to change, accept feedback, demonstrate high energy, and are accountable greatly increase your chances of victory!